New Hampshire
vs.
Vermont

SHEDD FREE LIBRARY
Washington, N.H.

Shedd Free Library was first established in 1867 from Sarah Shedd's entire estate of $2500. The building was built and donated to the town by Lumen T. Jefts in 1881.

Date: 7/29/98   Class: 974.2

NEW

New Hampshire
vs.
Vermont

SIBLING RIVALRY BETWEEN THE TWIN STATES

Edited
by
Lisa Shaw

Williams Hill Publishing
Grafton, New Hampshire

Printed in the United States of America
First Edition

ISBN 0-9652502-0-2
Cover design by The Image Connection, Inc./603-675-2303/www.imageconnection.com
Interior design by Karen Billipp, Eliot House Productions

For additional copies of this book, or for a catalog of our other New England titles, please write:

Williams Hill Publishing
RR 1 Box 1234
Grafton, New Hampshire 03240

To Mister Pippy, Rula Lenska, Miss Bunny, Allerton,
Sugar Bombe and Squatter, cats who sometimes make the
feud between New Hampshire & Vermont seem like a tea party.

Contents

Chapter One: Setting the Stage

New Hampshire vs. Vermont
by Judson Hale 3

Chapter Two: Ode to New Hampshire

A Good Friend
by Barbara Radcliffe Rogers 19

Why I Live in New Hampshire
by Judson Hale 23

The Politicos Speak
Senator Judd Gregg 25

Chapter Three: Love Song to Vermont

Vermont Won't Come to You
by Peter S. Jennison 31

Vermont Takes on the Man
by Chris Bohjalian 41

The Politicos Speak
Governor Howard Dean 45

Chapter Four: The Sparring Begins

The Quintessential New England Village—Where Is It?
by Lisa Shaw 51

Work in New Hampshire; Live in Vermont
by Ellen J. Bartlett 57

What New Hampshire and Vermont Have In Common:
A Dislike of Massachusetts
by Donna Dubuc 61

The View of Both States from the Top of a Mountain
by Tyler Resch 67

Driving on New Hampshire's Roads
by Tom Durgin 73

Vermont Drivers: Good Luck!
by Eric Roode 77

Chapter Five: The Gloves Come Off

Why I Hate New Hampshire
by Mike Barnicle 81

More of Why I Hate New Hampshire
by Mike Barnicle, again 85

Reasons for Hating Vermont
by Donald Hall 89

A Good Fight With a Long History
by Lisa Shaw 95

Chapter Six: An Uneasy Truce

Yankee Kingdom
by Ralph Nading Hill. 103

Acknowledgments 109

CHAPTER

ONE

Setting the Stage

*W*e think there is something special about being from New Hampshire. Vermonters feel the same about their state. About a decade ago the Vermont Legislature debated a bill that would officially declare the child of a couple living in Vermont to be a native, even if the child was born out of state. Part of the problem was too many Vermonters were going to hospitals across the river in New Hampshire to deliver. In the midst of the debate an old timer took the floor: "If the cat has kittens in the oven, that doesn't make them biscuits." It would take more than an act by the Legislature to make someone a native Vermonter.

—Hank Nichols,
Boston Globe, June 11, 1995

New Hampshire vs. Vermont

by
Judson Hale

THEY BORDER EACH OTHER, they look alike, and most outsiders have a hard time separating the two. Yet residents
know the differences are enormous.

They're like brothers who, as only the family knows,
couldn't be more different. With a landscape of open, rolling
farmland and small villages with white-steepled churches,
Vermont is the most rural state in the Union, according to
Census Bureau statistics. From an environmental point of
view, it's also the most politically liberal. New Hampshire, so
heavily forested that it was once described by Vermont's
Richard Ketchum as looking "like a summer camp that's
been closed for the winter," is the nation's fourth most
industrialized state and as politically conservative as any you
can name.

Geographically separated by the Connecticut River, they
lie next to each other in reverse, with each calling the other
an upside-down version of itself. New Hampshire, the

forty-fourth largest state in area, with about a million in population, is fattest at its bottom, which borders Massachusetts and, for eighteen miles, the sea. Landbound Vermont, half as big in population but slightly larger in area (ranking forty-third), is fattest at its top, which borders Canada. Surely no two brothers could grow up the same with such different hereditary characteristics.

"She's one of the two best states in the Union," wrote Robert Frost of New Hampshire, then added, "Vermont's the other." Frost can be excused for liking both states; after all, he was originally from California. Most people who know them well like one or the other. Not both.

New Hampshire seems to make people either proud (that number would consist exclusively of the state's residents) or angry (everyone else). Vermont, on the other hand, has a tendency to make people (particularly "flatlanders"—i.e., outsiders) either nostalgic or a little sick to their stomachs. The latter group consists of New Hampshire residents plus those few cynical Americans to whom the so-called New England image is vaguely repugnant.

There's little question that Vermont (particularly Vermont), Maine, Boston, and Cape Cod are, together, responsible for the New England image. New Hampshire just doesn't fit in. Former U.S. Senator Eugene McCarthy of Minnesota once said, "All New Hampshire is divided into three parts: Massachusetts, Maine, and Vermont." Putting aside the misconceptions inherent in that statement, it does demonstrate New Hampshire's lack of image. This, I submit, is unfair. New Hampshire is part of the New England image. It's just the part that people don't like.

For instance, consider how Dorothy Canfield Fisher, a writer and a Vermont summer person, described what she called "the Vermont tradition." She said it was "like the tang of an upland October morning, the taste of a drink from a cold mountain spring." Along the same lines, another writer, Craig Storti, found that "Vermont was the smell of grass after an April rain."

In contrast, there's a New Hampshire story (one of darned few, most New England stories being about Vermont or Maine) about a farmer (yes, just under one percent of New Hampshirites still farm) who was relaxing in his home with the evening newspaper. Finally, finding the soft April air, the sound of peepers, and the vapors of the damp, freshly plowed earth irresistible, he rose and headed for the front door. "Bessie," he called to his wife, "it's just too beautiful outside to stay in here. I'm going out and slaughter a hog."

If that doesn't help clarify the difference, contemplate for a moment a few of the things of which each state is proudest. Vermont points to its law banning highway billboards, its Act 250, which severely restricts real estate development, its generous aid to education and social services, and its basic general philosophy, written into the state constitution, that "private property ought to be subservient to public uses when necessity requires it." It is hardly insignificant that that document was based on the Quaker-influenced constitution of Pennsylvania.

New Hampshire would no more adopt the above measures or endorse that philosophy than it would elect Madeleine Kunin, Vermont's recent foreign-born, Jewish, Democratic woman governor, to the office of fence view-

er—or any office involving the spending of money. New
Hampshire glories in its frugality, rabidly protected by a four-
hundred-member General Court (the largest state legislature in the country) and the Governor's Council, a holdover
from the Royal Governor's Council, dedicated to keeping
the governor from doing anything foolish.

Like, for example, violating "The Pledge." Political candidates in New Hampshire, if they want a reasonable chance
of being elected, are expected to pledge they'll not support
anything faintly resembling a broad based state income tax.
New Hampshire's original bill of rights (taken from the busi-
ness-minded Puritans, except for religious and property
requirements) includes the right of revolution "whenever
the ends of government are perverted, and public liberty
manifestly endangered." The words "subservient to public
uses," as found in Vermont's constitution, don't appear anywhere in New Hampshire's. Excluding legislators themselves, New Hampshirites like the fact that the state has
retained its nineteenth-century pay scale for legislators too:
mileage, plus two hundred dollars every other year.
(Vermont pays its nearly two hundred legislators four hundred dollars for each week they're in session.)

Vermont has a few more heroes of which to be proud than
does New Hampshire. Ironically, almost all of them—Ethan
Allen, Calvin Coolidge, and the late Senator George Aiken,
for instance—personify that conservative, rock-ribbed
Republican sort of image Vermont once basked in for years.
And indeed, it used to be true. Vermont was the only state
in the country to vote straight Republican from the time the
Republican party began, in 1856, to 1962, when Vermonters

first elected a Democratic governor. (Even New Hampshire voted for FDR in 1936, 1940, and 1944.) When Senator Aiken advised President Johnson to declare victory in Vietnam and then bring the troops home, the nation smiled, not so much at his humor but more because he so perfectly personified the common-sense reputation of Vermonters.

New Hampshire's historical heroes are, for the most part, somewhat flawed or, worse, erroneously credited to Vermont. The only president to come from New Hampshire, Franklin Pierce, favored states' rights at exactly the worst time in American history to do so. Daniel Webster is a Granite Stater to be proud of, but unfortunately he moved permanently to Massachusetts halfway through his life.

New Hampshire's Revolutionary War hero, John Stark, is known mainly for his victory at the Battle of Bennington, Vermont. He's also credited with New Hampshire's official motto, "Live Free or Die," of which New Hampshirites are rather defiantly proud, while Vermonters and the national media enjoy it as the butt of jokes. (New Hampshire doesn't think much of Vermont's motto, "Freedom and Unity," either. How can you have both? they ask.)

John Stark's wife, Molly, is even more famous than her husband, but not in New Hampshire. Vermonters, inexplicably, seem inclined to name just about everything after her. There is a Molly Stark Trail, and there are Molly Stark schools, parks, gift shops (galore), streets, restaurants, and motels.

Vermont is proud it invented the first ski tow for downhill skiing (in 1934), while New Hampshire counters with its invention of the skimobile (1937). New Hampshire brags it has two Fortune 500 companies. Vermont brags it has none. And on it goes—each state always true to nothing but its character.

From time to time Vermont enjoys some modest national attention when someone sees "Champ," a Loch Ness-type monster in Lake Champlain, or perhaps one of the state's often-sighted-but-never-caught panthers. And its maple sugar/covered bridge image appears year in and year out in literature, advertisements, and even Bob Newhart's old television show. But New Hampshire eclipses all of that— briefly—every four years when it holds the nation's first presidential primary. For the weeks prior to that, New Hampshire is the center of attention in the nation—maybe even the world. And justifiably so, in the opinion of residents. "The state [of New Hampshire] is a better proving ground than most for an office seeker," wrote Nancy Coffey Heffernan and Ann Page Stecker in their 1986 book *New Hampshire*, "because . . . the voters there are not over-awed by politicians seeking public office."

It infuriates many outsiders, however, particularly members of the national media. The problem, I submit, stems from the fact they all arrive in New Hampshire thinking they're coming to Vermont. Then, since they never bother to learn the differences between the two states, the incongruities inherent in their basic misconceptions of New Hampshire make them angry. New Hampshire doesn't fit the story they've unconsciously written in their minds all their professional lives.

"New Hampshire is a fraud," wrote Henry Allen in February 1988 in the *Washington Post National Weekly*. He went on to rant about the nation being held hostage to a state made up of "souvenir hustlers, backwoods cranks, motorcycle racing fans . . . and tax-dodging Massachusetts suburbanites who have conspired . . . to create an illusion of noble, upright, granite-charactered sentinels of liberty out of little more than a self-conscious collection of bad (if beautiful) land, summer people, second-growth woods full of junked cars and decaying aristocracy, lakes howling with speedboats, state liquor stores that are open on Sundays, and the most vicious state newspaper in America, the Manchester *Union Leader*."

Poor fellow. Instead of finding Santa Claus in New Hampshire, as he was so sure he would, he found common, everyday reality. The covered bridges, maple syrup, Champ, and probably Santa Claus are over in Vermont, Mr. Allen.

Despite their contrasting natures, however, both New Hampshire and Vermont are proud of how they look. New Hampshire points to its seacoast, the Old Man of the Mountain (recently described by another irritated outside journalist as "possibly the least inspiring rock formation in America"), its lovely lakes, and the White Mountains, featuring Mount Washington. Vermont counters with its long shoreline on Lake Champlain, its Christmas-card countryside, and the Green Mountains, featuring Mount Mansfield. Vermonters hold Mount Mansfield in very high regard. A few years ago I gave a speech in a church outside Burlington in which I admired a large stained-glass window showing Jesus Christ rising to heaven, accompanied by a host of beautiful angels. In the background— there's no mistaking it—was Mount Mansfield.

The marked differences between these two brother states are really not surprising when you consider how each was brought up. Unlike most of the original colonists, New Hampshire's first settlers didn't arrive with an original charter, strong religious convictions, or a strong-willed proprietor like John Winthrop or Roger Williams. They were simply English adventurers, fishermen, and opportunists looking to make some money. This attitude fitted well with the Puritans in the neighboring Massachusetts Bay Colony, who, after a number of New Hampshire coastal towns came under Massachusetts jurisdiction during the mid-1600s, mixed their stern, frugal, conscientious, and ambitious approach to life with the New Hampshire settlers' self-reliance and independence.

New Hampshire today is still closely tied to Massachusetts in many ways. Tourists and second-homers in New Hampshire are principally Bay Staters. At the same time, New Hampshire abhors the very idea of "creeping Massachusettsism," a New Hampshire term that implies an assortment of liberal horrors, including higher taxes.

Although "discovered" by Samuel de Champlain on July 4, 1609, Vermont was settled more than a century later. The first settlers, mostly from Connecticut, arrived in the Brattleboro area in 1724. (Their declaration of independence called the territory New Connecticut, a name that had it not been changed within months, might well have destroyed the Vermont mystique before it began.) While New Hampshire was incorporating towns (60 percent of present-day New Hampshire towns were settled by 1775), clearing land, sending pine masts to England, and (aided by close proximity to the Boston market and ocean access) starting small industries that would grow into the major textile and shoe manufacturers of the nineteenth and early twentieth centuries, Vermont was floundering and in chaos.

This was due to some double-dealing by King George III. In effect, King George handed over Vermont to both New Hampshire and New York. He granted New Hampshire's governor, John Wentworth, all land to within thirty miles of the Hudson River and then turned around and gave New York the land all the way to the east bank of the Connecticut River. Massachusetts jumped in and claimed some of it too.

All this eventually led to Vermont's thumbing its nose at all its neighbors and everyone else too. In 1777, with Ethan Allen and his "Bennington Mob" leading the way, Vermont declared itself an independent state, answerable to nobody. Vermont remained independent until 1791, when it paid New York thirty thousand dollars to settle all its land disputes and was admitted to the Union.

Many of the New Hampshire claims in Vermont had been settled earlier by individual landowners, but the two states continued battling over their common boundary well into this century. They simply couldn't agree on making it the middle of the Connecticut River, as most neighboring states would do. Like brothers arguing over who should have the bigger piece of cake, they insisted on trying to pick one bank of the river as the boundary. Finally, in 1934, the matter went to the U.S. Supreme Court, which chose the west bank. New Hampshire, awarded the entire breadth of the river, felt it had won a victory until someone pointed out that the state would thus be responsible for maintaining all the bridges over the river. Score one for Vermont.

There *is* something historic on which Vermont and New Hampshire actually agree. Both maintain that the American Revolution did not begin at Concord and Lexington, Massachusetts, on April 19, 1775. New Hampshire favors December 13, 1774, when Major John Sullivan of the Granite State Volunteers and four hundred patriots attacked the British-held Fort William and Mary, at New Castle, New Hampshire. Vermont finds that particular action of no significance in the war's outcome and sees the Concord/Lexington fight as purely a defensive action. So it proudly points to Ethan Allen's capture of Fort Ticonderoga on May 10, 1775, as the first offensive action of the war. To be fair, I should say here that every New England state makes a case for having begun the American Revolution— with the exception of Maine, which ignores the Revolution and stoutly points out that it was settled well before the arrival of the Mayflower anyway.

Both states also claim to have played the primary roles in various battles that either strengthened or actually saved the Union. At Bunker Hill, New Hampshire's troops out-numbered the combined totals of Massachusetts and Connecticut, and Washington himself said the "bravery and resolution" of New Hampshire soldiers "far surpassed the other colonies." Vermont points to its role at Gettysburg almost ninety years later. Historians seem to agree that the actions of Stanhard's Vermont brigade were critical in repulsing Pickett's Charge at Gettysburg. Furthermore, Vermont can truthfully say it suffered more casualties in the Civil War, per capita, than any other state.

The most significant single reason for all the present-day differences between these two brother states, however, has nothing to do with political history. It has to do with the characteristics of the ground each inherited—the actual soil. Mark Twain said, "In the South, the people define the land and in the North, the land defines the people." Vermont's land has always been well-suited for farming, while New Hampshire's has not. With the exception of parts of the Connecticut and Merrimack river valleys, New Hampshire's soil consists mainly of glacial hardpan strewn with rocks and boulders. Thus, when the rural populations of both states were lured West by the discovery of gold in California, easier farming, and just plain Yankee restlessness, New Hampshire's lost population was more than made up for by immigrants, who, instead of battling with all those New Hampshire rocks, went to work in the growing factories and mills.

Except during the Civil War decade, New Hampshire's overall population steadily increased during the nineteenth century. Vermont, the region of New England least touched by industry, not only remained rural and agriculturally oriented, but its population declined during most of the same period. Even today Vermont has legally chartered towns, like Avery's Gore, Warner's Grant, Lewis, and Ferdinand, that remain virtually uninhabited.

In 1911, concerned by this loss of people, Vermont began its now-famous tourist industry—currently the number-one moneymaker in the state—by sending out the first state-sponsored tourist brochure. It was a profusely illustrated booklet of eighty pages entitled *Vermont, Designed by the Creator for the Playground of the Continent*.

Fourteen years later New Hampshire followed suit, although since the turn of the century it had been conducting

Old Home Day celebrations designed to bring back Western wanderers for at least a day. Its first tourist brochure was more modestly entitled *The Summer Playground of America.* Apparently that was more effective than Vermont's: the summer tourist business in the Granite State, luring people to huge hotels in the White Mountains and Lake Winnipesaukee region, grew by leaps and bounds while Vermont's increased much more slowly. There are those residents of New Hampshire today who wish it could have been the other way around.

The two states remain different. "You can feel the difference the minute you cross the Connecticut River," people say. But like brothers who tend to come together when threatened from outside, they face the future with similar concerns. The difference is in how they rank them. New Hampshire, alarmed by its recent economic slowdown after a decade of incredible growth fueled by its high-tech industries, is still afraid some political sleaze will eventually succeed in getting a state income tax passed. But economic and development pressures and the resulting changing character of many of its communities are growing concerns as well. Steady pressure to increase controls statewide flies directly in the face of the historic home-rule philosophy, which placed the responsibility of decision making mostly in the hands of individual towns.

Vermont is afraid of economic and development pressures too. In fact, that's its primary concern. But it's a concern that goes further than being apprehensive, as New Hampshire is, about the changing character of its individual communities. To most Vermonters, these pressures threaten, as they put it, "our way of life." As the only New Englanders (with the possible exception of some in Maine) who actually live the New England image, they want to continue to do so.

However, there's a new type of pressure growing steadily in Vermont these days, and it's not without some irony. It is made up of Vermonters who adamantly oppose anything that could result in higher taxes and who want Vermont businesses (like IBM and the Digital Equipment Corporation up in the Burlington area, for instance), to expand. "Vermont is on the extreme end of environmental issues," said Dick Tanch, former general manager of the Mount Mansfield ski area, recently, "and it's detrimental to our economic health."

So while there's pressure in New Hampshire to be more like Vermont, there's pressure in Vermont to be more like New Hampshire—just like brothers who've had their differences but who are getting along in years.

CHAPTER

TWO

Ode to New Hampshire

S *eems there was this old Vermont farmer who lived along the Vermont/New Hampshire border. He was a fifth-generation Vermonter and the farm had been in the family for almost as long.*

Well it seems that one day some government surveyors came through his property, doing some routine surveying work for the state. About a week later he gets this letter from the state telling him that his farm isn't in Vermont after all, but is actually on the New Hampshire side of the border. Well, folks in town found out about this and thought it was the funniest thing they ever heard of; all this time him thinking he was a Vermonter when he wasn't. The next time he was at the general store, his old friends started to tease him something fierce. The old farmer turned to his tormentors and says, "You know, I'm just as happy that I don't live in Vermont after all."

"Now why's that, Eben?"

"Well at my age, I just don't know if I could have stood another one of those Vermont winters!"

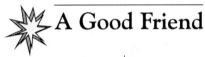 A Good Friend

by

Barbara Radcliffe Rogers

IF NEW HAMPSHIRE WERE A PERSON, instead of a piece of real estate, it would be one of my best friends. After all, we've shared a great many of life's pleasures and its company never disappoints me. It is endearing in a way that endures, comfortable and familiar, but with enough surprises to keep it interesting.

My earliest childhood memories are set here. I can't remember the first time I saw the ocean or splashed in its icy waves, but it was on a New Hampshire beach. The first mountain I climbed was Potash, the first slopes I skied were Cranmore's, the first trout I caught was in the Zealand River ... the list is endless. I came back here to be married, and here we chose to raise our children, so they could enjoy the same childhood pleasures we had.

I've lived and traveled in many other parts of the world, and much as I loved my neighborhood in Verona, Italy, or on Beacon Hill, New Hampshire never stopped being home. I

sat on alpine mountain sides and wrote poetry about birch-
es on granite hills. If I was never exactly homesick, I never
forgot where home was, either.

What is there about this small state that makes it such an
enduring friend? Its diversity, for one thing. Its landscapes
rise from the tidal pools of Rye, over the rolling, lake-stud-
ded hills, to the treeless peaks of the mountains I climbed
every summer. Look twice at any of those landscapes and
you'll rarely find it looking the same. Four distinct seasons,
which we New Englanders take for granted, but which
much of the world do not share, paint each scene in a whole
palette of different colors every few months, from white to
green, to red and gold, to brown.

Beyond the visual picture is the dimension of a rich history. Often, the whole panoply of that history is told in a single place—Odiorne Point was one of New England's earliest
settlements, and in a short walk there you can see reminders
of three centuries of coastal life, from an early salt-water
farm to the giant earth mounds that hid World War II
defenses.

That history is lively and colorful largely because of the
people who lived it. The challenges of its terrain, weather
and soil have given New Hampshire people a unique character—or perhaps independent and self-sufficient people
have been attracted to its challenges and have met them
head-on.

Whether the land made the people or the people chose
the land, no one denies that New Hampshire has spawned
an independent lot of native sons and daughters. Some call
it gritty, and not without cause. For one thing, we usually say
exactly what we think. And we rarely mumble it, either.

We balance this up-frontedness with our opinions by making it nearly impossible to tell anything else about us, least of all from our appearances. A family's net worth often bears no relation to the size of their home or make of their car. Like Boston ladies and their hats, we don't buy our homes, we have them. We may have had them for generations, and the beautiful four-square Colonial may be all that's left of a family fortune, stately and well-kept by sweat alone, on diminished acreage and mortgaged to its eaves. On the other hand that little cottage with the slightly unkempt hedge may be the home of our local millionaire. We tend to live in what we have—or in what we like.

Just as you can't tell people by their cover, you can't tell places by theirs. A restaurant that looks like a road house may have a chef lately arrived from a trendy city restaurant, turning out meals that look like a center-fold from Gourmet. And the nondescript local museum may have priceless antiques and a curator or docent with a Ph.D. in that period. These surprises are as much a part of New Hampshire as "Bump" signs and moose beside the roads. It makes each new day here an adventure, even for natives.

New Hampshire's ethnic diversity—it is far more varied than its neighbors on either side—comes as a surprise to many who expect a solid wall of old Yankee-ness. But even its ethnicity is of its own peculiar stripe, partly because the state is the quintessential melting pot. My friend with the Irish name is really half Greek and half Italian. Her Irish name comes from her husband, whose maternal grandmother is French Canadian. Are you still with me? The wedding dances may be Lebanese or the polka, but however blurred the ethnic lines may become, something of the old traditions remain. And the next generation, although they eat pork pie, not apple pie, for breakfast, often seems more Yankee than the old blue blood.

So when I introduce you to my old friend New Hampshire, don't try to figure her out. Just enjoy her good company, marvel at her good looks, and revel in all the little surprises each new encounter brings. I think you'll agree, after you get to know her that familiarity breeds love. And if it doesn't,   like the bumper sticker says, "Visit New Hampshire...Then go home."

✳ Why I Live in New Hampshire

by

Judson Hale

I LIVE IN NEW HAMPSHIRE. Not "so I can get a better view of Vermont," as Maxfield Parrish once said, but rather because it's both where I work and where I want to be. Yes, it's an exasperating sort of state. The New Hampshire state representative Deborah ("Arnie") Arnesen of Orford describes it as having a "tax-free, self-serving, if-you-can-make-it-you-can-keep-it" economic philosophy, and there's truth to that. As with most residents, New Hampshire makes me angry—and proud. I don't like reading that only children under eighteen and adults "in pain" can receive Medicaid dental care. Or that New Hampshire remains the last state in the nation without mandated kindergarten. I'm embarrassed that our state doesn't recognize Martin Luther King Day specifically by name. I'm irritated at having to celebrate Memorial Day on a different day of the week from the rest of America. To tell you the truth, I'm amazed New

Hampshire can see its way clear to go along with the international time zones.

But I'm proud to be a resident of a state that best exemplifies so many of the legendary characteristics of the mystical New Englander, even those not always considered by some to be attractive. I'm speaking of frugality, fierce independence, shrewd business sense, ingenuity—and not just a little pride. And to think it has all these New England qualities and more without ever being credited, as Vermont is in spades, with contributing to the New England image!

And Vermont? Well, up in West Glover I have relatives who have farm animals and tap their maple trees for the pure joy of it—and a few more in Woodstock, a town supported by (and, behind the scenes, run by) the Rockefellers. A few of my dearest New York friends have vacation homes outside Grafton, a town preserved by the Windham Foundation. A large part of the foundation's money annually earmarked for Grafton comes from a charitable trust established in 1962 by the family of a very caring New York society lady, a Mrs. Rodney Fiske, following her death. She summered in Grafton and was fond of describing the town as "the little village in the hills."

Yes, Vermont is lovely. A lovely state to visit. Quaint too.

The Politicos Speak
Senator Judd Gregg

IN DECEMBER OF 1995, Senator Judd Gregg wrote a letter to the Click and Clack brothers on the National Public Radio show, Car Talk. Here we join the show in progress

Click: I have on occasion said some nasty things about New Hampshire. They're wackos up there.

Click then proceeds to read aloud a letter from Senator Judd Gregg that the senator had sent to the brothers:

Senator Gregg: In recognizing that this assault by individuals that live in a state that has a dead fish as its symbol—Massachusetts, is that right?—and whose population regularly migrates to New Hampshire to purchase all nature of tax-free goods, to ski and go to the lakes and breathe fresh air, one should not take seriously these barbs which obviously derive from simple jealousy.

However, buried within your tortured discourse you did pose one excellent question. Why are Maine, Vermont, and New Hampshire so different when "just a line on a piece of paper separates them?" Let me explain and I'll keep it simple.

Vermont, if you will refer back to your map, is obviously upside-down. Need I say more? Maine is a more complicated case dealing with the ratio of moose to people and the interaction thereof for several generations. I refer you to any number of Steven King novels, a Maine resident, for primary source material.

New Hampshire, however, as most people from the former socialist commune to our south know, is the lowest taxed state in the country. No income or sales tax. With the best health care, highest SAT scores, and most livable environment in the nation, all ratings achieved from independent NPR-recognized sources.

In addition, we have more cars per capita than any other state in the country, which means any mechanic with half a mind (that's redundant) would be living and working in New Hampshire rather than Massachusetts. But you already know that.

Clack: Well, he didn't say that the cars were *drivable*.

Gregg: All this having been said, I regret to inform you that I have referred this matter to my New Hampshire attorneys How Do We Cheat 'Em, whose slower and more expensive cousins practice in your building and in your state. You should hear from them in due course.

Pending that, could you please tell me why the check engine on my Ford Taurus does not go off? And yes, I checked the engine.

Sincerely,
Judd Gregg,
U.S. Senator from New Hampshire

CHAPTER

THREE

Love Song to Vermont

*T*wo guys from New Hampshire were traveling in the Midwest. One night, they went barhopping, and the minute they opened their mouths, everyone wanted to know where they were from.

"New Hampshire," they answered.

"Where's that?" everyone wanted to know.

They tried to explain the geographic location of New Hampshire several times, all in vain. But they finally figured out the correct way to answer the question.

The next time, the exchange went like this:

"Where you from?"

"New Hampshire."

"Where's that?"

"In Vermont."

Vermont Won't Come to You

by

Peter S. Jennison

*Vermont is perhaps the only place in America a
stranger can feel homesick for—before
he has even left it.*

—Neil R. Pearce, *The New England States*

OF ALL THE FOLKLORIC JOKES ABOUT motorists asking directions from stolid old-timers in Vermont ("Does this road go
to Greensboro?....Nope; stays right here," et al), the most
revealing may be this:

"Does it matter which road I take to Montpelier?" asks
the puzzled traveler confronting a choice of routes.

The grizzled codger on the stoop of the general store
regards the stranger skeptically, "Not to me it don't."

"The Switzerland of North America," as British historian
Lord Bryce called it eighty-five years ago, clings tenaciously
to many of the maverick characteristics cultivated during its

fourteen years as an independent Republic between 1777 and 1791. Though many of the old-fashioned Norman Rockwell traditions are fading (post-war immigration has nearly homogenized the distinctive nasal twang of the Vermont accent that so amuses Southerners, for instance), the state remains "Contrary Country," to borrow the title of one of Ralph Nading Hill's historical profiles of the state.

Vermonters are as chauvinistic, in their way, as Texans (who also once boasted of their republic): no matter where in the world the sons and daughters of Vermont happen to be living, they regard themselves as Vermonters—not Floridians or Californians. This born-again Vermonter (I returned to my native heath after twenty-five years elsewhere) always used to introduce himself on the lecture circuit as a Vermonter—"like being from Missouri, only more so."

What accounts for this durable mystique? The answer lies in an adhesive compound of geography, original patterns of settlement, an aggressive defense of territorial integrity, vigorous self-government, ingenuity, and a high degree of tolerance for the right of other people to be eccentric or misguided.

Vermont's not just a land of milk, marble, maple syrup and "white gold." Along the highways and byways explored in this book, the mobile or chair-bound traveler can retrace the course of the state's dramatic birth, growth, and achievements, from Revolutionary Bennington to Burlington, the "Queen City," which now resembles a smaller Boston as the state's financial, educational, medical, and communications center. Burlington recently became the state's only 100,000-plus Standard Metropolitan Area.

Here, too, one can meet many of the more colorful and uncommon individuals who influenced the life and times of the state and, indeed, America itself: the Rabelasian free-thinker, Ethan Allen, and his crafty brother, Ira, who led the Green Mountain Boys in guerilla warfare against the Hampshiremen, Yorkers, and "the cruel ministereal tools of George ye Third"; railroad builders like Charles Paine and Frederick Billings; capitalists "Jubilee Jim Fisk," the robber baron who was martyred for love, and Hetty Green, the richest woman in turn-of-the-century America; educators Emma Willard and John Dewey; soldiers and statesmen of the caliber of Admiral George Dewey and Senator George D. Aiken; the protean George Perkins Marsh, ecologist and diplomat; two United States presidents; writers, painters and sculptors of international renown; and inventors like John Deere, maker of the plow that broke the plains. Vermont thus appeals to the tourist who likes to see new places without sacrificing the comforts of home, as well as the inquisitive traveler who wants to know what lies behind the brick and frame facades.

After two hundred years of statehood, Vermont is being colonized at a faster pace than all of New England in the 17th century. Still among the smallest in the Union with a population of 550,000 and represented in Congress by a lone Representative, the Green Mountain State is suffering acute growing pains. Many of the most articulate post-World War II refugees from megapolitan centers—unflatteringly called "flatlanders"—are now making common cause with the native "woodchucks" who deplore the invasion of well-heeled condomaniacs and the proliferation of asphalt jungle shopping malls. Even the spiritual descendants of Ethan and

Ira Allen, the biggest land speculators of the 1760s, are supporting legislation designed to stem the erosion of the farm land and forests being avidly devoured to satisfy the major ski resorts' insatiable appetite for Lebensraum.

But Vermont lies within two hours' drive of some 35 million people, and if they choose to make the state a playground, there isn't much contemporary Green Mountain Boys can do about it, short of adopting a stockade mentality.

Attitudes and political behavior as well as weather are affected by the Green Mountains, born in the mists of the Cambrian Age 425 million years ago, and more recently— from one million to 12,000 years—ground down by recurrent glaciers, which reduced Mount Mansfield, the highest peak, from 12,000 feet at birth to 4,393. To Westerners, the Green Mountains are not especially impressive. Some relatives of the author's visiting from Colorado asked where they were. "You've just driven through them," I replied. "Oh. You call those hills mountains?"

Still, they loom large in Vermont history and way of life. As Ethan Allen once said, "The gods of the hills are not the gods of the valleys," a pronouncement more prescient than he knew. One political application was the "mountain rule," which, for nearly 150 years, decreed that the top elective offices should be held alternately by Westerners and Easterners. Residents of the Connecticut River corridor were likely to be more conservative than those of the Lake Champlain Valley, and before the proliferation of railroad links in the middle of the nineteenth century, East-West communications were spotty. Stone-strewn hill farms really flourished only during the heyday of pointynose sheep raising, as compared to the verdant dairy farms in the broad Champlain basin and along the northern border with Canada.

One of our droll humorists, the late Allen Foley, used to tell this story of the man "from away" watching a farmer at the tedious chore of carting stones from his corn field.

"What are you doing?"

"Pickin' stone."

"Where did all those stones come from?"

"Glacier brought 'em."

"Where did the glacier go?"

"Back for more stone."

The mountains and their "white gold" have sustained Vermont's economy ever since the mid-1930 Depression years when Woodstock and Stowe became the ski capitals of the East. And thousands of magnificent public buildings from Washington to Riyadh have been wrested from virtually inexhaustible veins of marble and granite.

Our topography, moreover, has helped "to perpetuate ruralism as the essential social condition," according to Frank Bryan, author of the scholarly *Yankee Politics in Rural Vermont* (1974), and comic *Real Vermonters Don't Milk Goats*. The growth of Vermont was defined by "the homestead and the hamlet." Nearly everywhere a hill lies across the path of togetherness. "For people to live apart from one another among Vermont's never-ending hills is as natural as people living close to one another around New York's harbor, at St. Louis's midwest prairie divide, or on Denver's plateau." The ex-urban gentry who have moved to Vermont in recent years are willing to pay dearly for ruralism because there's so little of it left elsewhere. At the same time, ruralism has honed a "special community ethic...bonds of communal spirit that are very likely matched by few other states."

This bonding is dramatized every March by town meetings, where questions of local self-governance are debated and usually resolved in remarkable displays of civility. Controversial public issues frequently churn to the surface: in 1982, for example, nearly all town meetings in Vermont adopted resolutions supporting a mutual U.S.-U.S.S.R. freeze on the testing, production, and deployment of nuclear weapons.

Public life is, largely, branded by personalism, tolerance, and a sense that the state's social fabric and government are still on a scale small enough to be both workable and humane. Our legislature is the least venal in the nation. In the last twenty years, the century-old Republican political monopoly has been broken by three Democratic governors (Philip Hoff, Thomas Salmon, and Madeleine Kunin), by U.S. Senator Patrick Leahy, and by a current Democratic majority in the legislature—further evidence of independent thinking.

Unlike other northern New England states, Vermont graduated from an agrarian to semi-technological society without being affected by the industrial revolution—from "cow-chips to micro-chips," as U.V.M. professor of Business Administration Ronald Savitt puts it. Although hydropower is plentiful and once fueled the woolen mills on the Winooski River, the early machine tool factories of

Springfield on the Black River, as well as innumerable grist
and saw mills along smaller streams (and remains a significant link in today's electrical power grid), Vermont was virtually untouched by the reverberations of industrialism.
While dairy farming has declined drastically in the past
decade, we remain an essentially agrarian society.

As the market for fluid milk shrank, cheese makers began
to prosper, and other Vermont-made comestibles—smoked
ham and bacon, preserves, honey-mustards, chocolates and
maple sugar products—are being exported to upscale stores
in New York and Boston. Ben & Jerry's ice cream, first con-
cocted in a Burlington store-front, has gone national.

Vermont's hospitality, too, has become sophisticated.
Luxurious country inns and four-star restaurants can be
found in almost every town, many of them staffed by graduates of the New England Culinary Institute in Montpelier.

Education and health care have achieved high standards.
Most towns are now willing to fund above-average schools.
The University of Vermont is supplemented by a state college system. Private institutions are flourishing: Norwich
University has transcended its military academy origins;
Middlebury, Bennington, and Marlboro radiate excellence;
Goddard College was in the vanguard of free-spirited learn-
ing techniques, just as the Putney School has been at the
secondary level. Special education for handicapped stu-
dents has had a high priority; many post-war settlers were
attracted by the state's enlightened programs for develop-
mentally disabled children.

The good old country doctor who made house calls in his
gig or Model T coupe has disappeared into the vortex of
modern medicine, but probably the best medical center

north of Boston grows in Burlington; the larger towns have well-equipped hospitals. In Manchester and other resorts, walk-in clinics serve ailing or damaged vacationers; and most communities have fast-squad rescue units as alert and dedicated as their volunteer fire department colleagues.

Natives swear that crossing the border into Vermont induces a subtle change of atmosphere. One's spirits mysteriously rise. Visiting motorists and cyclists begin to notice a vague sense of loss; something is missing. Billboards! Alone among the states, Vermont has banned all off-premise advertising signs, great and small, since 1968—another tangible reminder of the Green Mountain state's contrariness. The once-controversial measure came to symbolize Vermonters' determination to preserve the unadulterated landscape of mountains, lakes, farmland and forests without the distracting intrusion of monstrous ads for personal hygiene, cigarettes, beverages, cars, restaurants and motels.

As a compromise, standardized directional signs for some tourist attractions are posted discreetly along state highways. After twenty years, some innkeepers—and, indeed, a few travelers—grumble, but the great majority of residents and visitors applaud the billboard ban as refreshing to the eye and spirit.

The anti-billboard movement was born in the thirties. In a 1937 letter to the *Rutland Herald*, Dorothy Thompson, the newspaper correspondent then married to Sinclair Lewis and living in Barnard, wrote: "I noticed this summer, and to my horror and dismay, that the billboard scourge, which has ruined the landscape of half of the United States, is spreading to Vermont. Won't the citizens of Vermont unite to protest?

"If aesthetic considerations do not move us, let us consider the matter from the standpoint of cold cash. Vermont has beauty to sell. Thousands and thousands of tourists come here every summer, for no other reason than that Vermont is lovely. They can see billboards from Connecticut to California. The absence of them is a positive asset."

Vermonters tend to unite with ail deliberate speed, but her letter lent impetus to what the Vermont Association for Billboard Restriction was doing at the time. State Representative Horace Brown of Springfield, an artist, fathered legislation requiring the licensing of billboards, restricting their size and specifying the distance they were to be removed from the highway.

Challenges to this law were rejected by the Vermont Supreme Court in 1942. In the 1950s and 60s, Colonel Fairfax Ayers of Shaftsbury and his Vermont Roadside Council lobbied hard for the stronger legislation eventually enacted by a sharply-divided legislature in 1968, for which State Representative Ted Riehle is credited.

Vermont again made environmental news in 1972 by becoming the second state (after Oregon) to ban non-returnable bottles and cans, noticeably reducing roadside litter in annual Green-Up days.

In the post-World War II years, Vermonters continued to boast how they had reaffirmed their independence by rejecting the Green Mountain Parkway, but they could also boast more miles of federal highway per square mile than any other state in the union. In 1953 Governor Emerson pledged his administration to "a policy of matching all available Federal funds" for road construction, which proceeded apace; and in

1956 moved vigorously to take full advantage of the federally-financed construction of interstate highways I-91 and I-89 as "the very core of Vermont's future development." To secure funding for this expansion, particularly of state highway feeder routes, the state abandoned its "pay as you go" tradition and substituted bond issues.

Vermonters have had to make concessions to the pressures and realities of the late 1980s, some more grudging than others, but the character of the countryside that Bernard DeVoto described as "every American's second home" remains relatively intact, thanks in part to pioneering land-use legislation designed to control growth. As Ralph Nading Hill, the late historian, wrote in *Yankee Kingdom*, our valley towns, "white and serene, seem to have become a universal symbol of nostalgia—of belonging somewhere....The reason is, perhaps, that the people of a rootless age find something admirable about a slice of hillcountry that has resisted being made over into the latest fashionable image."

Finally, as the landscape painter Luigi Lucione remarked, "Vermont is beautiful but not romantic. You have to go to it—it won't come to you."

Vermont Takes on the Man

by

Chris Bohjalian

SOMETIMES I'M JEALOUS OF NEW HAMPSHIRE.

I know that coming from the mouth of a Vermonter those words are the worst sort of blasphemy.

But it's true. Sometimes I really am jealous of my neighbors across a river to the east, and it's not simply because their license plates exude the macho fervor of the American Revolution: "Live Free or Die."

Nor is it because there's no sales tax in New Hampshire, or because my neighbors there buy their wine in state liquor stores bigger than Fenway Park.

It's not even because New Hampshire has the first presidential primary every four years, the first chance to turn hopefuls into has-beens, or elevate never-weres into also-rans.

No, I'm jealous of New Hampshire because of its state symbol: an old man made of granite, with a chin stronger than Dick Tracy's.

Sometimes that's what I think we need here in Vermont. Not the warm and toasty foliage motif we have now, not our pastoral Green Mountain fluff.

We need something to complete with a guy with a chin made of rock, something—or someone—to take on New Hampshire's Old Man of the Mountain. And while Thomas Salmon, a former governor and the current president of the University of Vermont, has the requisite strong, square Brian-Dennehy-like jaw, I don't think he's the type to pose for a license plate logo.

Consequently, here are four Vermonters we should put in the ring with the old man, and use to bolster state spirit, dress up our highway rest areas, and merchandise on tawdry T-shirts for flatlanders.

CHAMP. Lake Champlain's very own Loch Ness sort of monster, our frequently sighted (though rarely filmed), frolicking version of Puff. Granted, the southern half of the state might lobby against Champ, arguing that if we're going to use a slimy reptilian monster with scales, we should choose instead the Las Vegas developers who want to turn the defunct dog track in Pownal into a casino. They may be right.

And I also realize that we might have to battle New York for the rights to exploit Champ. Champ is, after all, practically the only tourist attraction left in some of the half-deserted little towns on Lake Champlain's New York shore. So be it. Port Henry can have custody of the monster during ski season, but we get him (her?) on Bennington Battle Day.

BERNARD SANDERS. I know he wears glasses and he wasn't even born here. But as all the biographies of

Burlington's first socialist mayor (and the state's current Congressman) make clear, Bernie is one tough hombre. If any guy can knock the stuffing and steel-reinforced supports out of the Old Man of the Mountain, it's Bernie Sanders.

THE OFFICIAL B.S.T. BOVINE. BST—known affectionately by its friends as bovine somatotropin—turns an ordinary Holstein or Jersey into Super Cow, that cud-chewing crusader for dairy justice. While I understand that the possible long-term effects of bovine growth hormone on people and cows still worry a great many milk drinkers, anything with the name bovine somatotropin has got to be pretty potent. Pump enough of it into one of our Vermont cows, and I'd be willing to bet we could produce the Arnold Schwarzenegger of dairy deliverance.

WAL-MART. Talk about things that take a licking and keep on ticking, talk about life after death. Never has a store been so determined to weather bad publicity, battle grass roots opposition, and boldly go where no mass merchandiser has gone before—smack into the midst of the white steeples, rolling meadows, and rural idyll we call Vermont. Wal-Mart is here, the proof that not even Kathie Lee Gifford can generate a sufficiently bad taste (saccharine or sweat shop) in our mouths to keep cheap jeans at least one state away.

And it seems to me that if you're battling a hunk of rock in New Hampshire that has survived for centuries, a slab of stone that has outlasted acid rain and John Sununu, you have to respect the sheer staying power and determination of the developers behind Vermont's very first Wal-Marts.

The Politicos Speak
Governor Howard Dean

GOVERNOR HOWARD DEAN APPEARED as a speaker on New Hampshire Public Radio's morning news show called "The Exchange" with host Laura Knoy to speak on a number of issues, including the ongoing feud between New Hampshire and Vermont. Here's the exchange:

Laura Knoy: Vermont and New Hampshire are different in their philosophy and politics. Why?

Governor Howard Dean: Historically, I don't know the answer to that. I can talk about recent times. A lot of the population for both of our states are immigrants from elsewhere—New York, Massachusetts, Connecticut—both got very different kinds of immigrants. People moved to Vermont to get away from the big cities and to have a more open kind of communication with their fellow human beings. An awful lot of the public in New Hampshire, particularly southern New Hampshire, left Mass. to escape high taxes and to have a more suburban lifestyle. And their motivations are very different. So I think there are tax kinds of differences.

I think New Hampshirites are less tolerant of government intrusion and taxes, versus Vermont, which doesn't like government intrusion and taxes but is willing to think about it as a possible option in some cases. That differential has to do with the folks that have moved in since the 1960s.

New Hampshire has a history of being tight-fisted at the state level but at the local level they're very generous. Their property tax is the highest in the country by far and that's 'cause local people are willing to shell out for their neighbors. I think the public in Vermont is not, I mean they may be fiscally conservative and I am too, but I don't think they're mean-spirited or tight-fisted and I think they will take care of their neighbors.

The other differential really, I think, is sort of a historical political accident. During the Depression, we tended toward a more central government. People like George Aiken might have been Democrats if they lived today. The Democratic Party didn't exist in Vermont for 109 years. Vermont was one of the two states that voted for Alf Landon during the 1936 election, the other being Maine. New Hampshire voted for FDR. That time, you had two wings of the Republican Party and the so-called Aiken-Gibson ring gained ascendancy. They were the more populist wing; they were against the utilities and the bankers, which is a different wing of the party, and they alternated back and forth in terms of ascendancy and the governorship. But the Aiken-Gibson wing really gained ascendancy and they were really concerned with the needs of ordinary working people. In the absence of a Democratic Party with that in their platform, that was left to the Aiken-Gibson wing. And that's where you get the social tolerance and social support systems that we see today. Obviously that was very much refined by Phil Hoff, who was the first Democratic governor in 109 years, and I think probably the most pivotal figure in the state in the last century who brought us into the modern era. But I think the groundwork was really laid by the so-called Gibson-Aiken wing, the Republican Party, between the 1930s end the 1950s.

And that didn't happen in New Hampshire. In New Hampshire, even though initially they were more inclined to vote Democratic in the 1930s, their entire political culture centered around local government doing for their own people And the state never obtained the kind of ascendancy that it did because of the Republican differences of opinion inside the Republican Party in Vermont.

Knoy: What is Vermont's relationship with New Hampshire?

Governor Dean: A friendly rivalry. We've had a lot of fun at each other's expense over the years. I actually spent a lot to time in New Hampshire because my favorite thing in life is canoeing down the Connecticut River, 90 percent of which is in New Hampshire, although we take care to camp on the Vermont side. Actually we camp on both sides. The northern part of

New Hampshire is spectacularly beautiful; the southern part is much more developed and is not something that I hope to see happen in Vermont to that degree. The two states have a very good relationship although we are very different and we certainly have a very strong and sometimes intense rivalry.

CHAPTER

FOUR

The Sparring Begins

New Hampshire

She's one of the two best states in the Union

Vermont's the other. And the two have been

Yokefellows in the sap yoke from of old

In many Marches. And they lie like wedges,

Thick end to thin end and thin end to thick end,

And are a figure for the way the strong

Of mind and strong of arm should fit together,

One thick where one its thin and vice versa.

The Vermont mountains stretch extended straight,

New Hampshire mountains curl up in a coil.

—Robert Frost

The Quintessential New England Village—Where Is It?

by

Lisa Shaw

I'D BEEN DRIVING BY A LITTLE GIFT SHOP located in the barn of a house on Route 4 in my town of Grafton, New Hampshire, since it had opened for business three years before. I'd seen the sign for "La Vie En Rose," as it was called, many times before, and more often than not, it was closed when I had time to stop by, or open when I was already late on my way to someplace else.

One day, the planets finally aligned and I pulled into the driveway. I proceeded to step into a shop that combined hand-thrown pottery with Victorian picture frames all slammed up against the coolness of the fieldstones that held up this former chicken barn.

Three minutes after I had walked through the door of the shop—the barn was attached to the owner's house, and once she knew someone was in the shop, it took her awhile to get there—Joni appeared and we began to chat. She had a calmness and serenity that added a homeyness to the shop. A few teenagers from the innards of the barn occasionally appeared to ask a few questions before flitting away again.

As we were talking, the front door of the shop opened, throwing a sudden light onto the dark, cozy space. A man and a woman from away, probably Massachusetts, entered. I don't know what it is about people who alight in Grafton for a few minutes before moving on to more commodious, beckoning towns, but their aura of clothes, hair and shoes that are newer than mine, give them away every time. With the men, well, they lack a certain scruffiness that musters respect from residents here, as well as oil or dirt stains indelibly etched onto their pants a few years previous. But with the women, the roots of their hair is what gives them away. I regularly let my hair color appointments slide until my roots appear like a skunk in reverse on the top of my head. The guy who's done my hair for quite a few years now always clucks his tongue at me when I come in and inevitably tries to talk me into a shorter, more stylish—for somewhere else—creation than the shoulder-length part-down-the-middle that I've come to favor for its simplicity in the last few years. Though at this point still, he goes through his obligatory spiel as an inside joke with me—someday I'll tell him, "Yes," and he'll probably keel over from shock.

Anyway, the couple-from-away made their way down the granite steps and into the shop, blinking vigorously as their eyes grew used to the dark.

They looked around, located the two humans standing at the counter by the sounds of our voices, and then in a loud clear voice, asked us how to find Grafton Village.

I already knew where this was leading; I went first. "What are you looking for?" I asked.

The woman fairly moved as if she was fluffing up her peafeathers with pride over this, her journey through unspoiled America. "We've been told that Grafton is the quintessential New England village," she proclaimed. I had to stifle a laugh. You see, I speak to a lot of people on the phone each week, and when I give them my address, at least one says, "Oh, I spent the night in Grafton once. It's a beautiful place, isn't it?"

What the woman in the shop and the people on the phone are inevitably referring to is Grafton, *Vermont,* not New Hampshire. It's a common-enough mistake in these parts. You see, my Grafton is not quaint, it's a no-nonsense town where two of the three general store buildings in town were built from utilitarian cinder blocks, and the one of these buildings that is still open heats with a newfangled pellet stove and has an RCA pizza-sized satellite dish perched on the roof, with the store TV tuned to Ricki Lake or Oprah or such from the time the front door is unlocked until it's closed up again fifteen hours later. Neither a pot-bellied stove nor a pair of grizzled old men bent over a barrel playing checkers and bemoaning the loss of the good ol' days in incomprehensible Yankee are anywhere to be found.

Grafton, Vermont, on the other hand, is a shrewdly recreated village with gaslights, no visible power lines, and a raft of 200-year-old buildings that were propped up with millions of outside dollars back in the 1960s so that the town could rightfully vie for this day, more than three decades later, when an idealistic, nostalgic thirtysomething couple from Dedham, Massachusetts, driving a new George Jetson Ford Taurus could refer to the town in hushed voices as "the quintessential New England village."

Of course, when early townspeople were casting around for suitable names for their newfound frontier towns north and west of Boston, they probably didn't have a clue back then that their acts would so confuse later day explorers. However, it can't solely be coincidence—or laziness—that's responsible for the towns of Springfield, Grafton, Orange, Plainfield, and a slew of other identical names that were granted to towns in adjacent counties that were settled around the same time.

There's always the story that I've heard about the desk clerks at the Woodstock Inn in Woodstock, Vermont, and the Woodstock Inn in Woodstock, New Hampshire, being on a first-name basis with each other due to the more than a few tourists who proceed bravely to their destinations only to be told that they're in the wrong state.

As for the couple in the gift shop, they appeared a bit crestfallen when I suggested they head for Woodstock, Vermont, which every guidebook writer refers to as The Quintessential New England Town.

"Oh, but we've just come from there," the man offered, probably thinking that Woodstock, Vermont, wasn't quintessential enough. Indeed, the vacation industry in New England and elsewhere has turned us into a nation of superlative seekers, making us feel as though we've failed if we haven't experienced the best of everything there is to see in our travels.

So we pointed them down the road to New London, populated and with sidewalks for the uninitiated. And no cinder blocks anywhere that were visible to the naked eye.

✳ Work in New Hampshire; Live in Vermont

by

Ellen J. Bartlett

DAN FRASER REMEMBERS WHEN HE was a small boy working at the general store, watching the farmers as they drove their horses down Main Street.

Fraser is 73 now. He owns the general store. He still watches the traffic. But a different breed of commuter passes through town, doctors and accountants and university professors, heading for the little bridge over the Connecticut River.

"They're moving here hand over fist," he said from the back of Dan and Whit's. "On account of that school over there. "

Dartmouth College may have drawn these people to work in Hanover, New Hampshire, but something else sent them house hunting on the other side of the river.

Almost a third of Dartmouth's 2,600-plus employees live in Vermont, according to the college, a quarter of those in

Norwich. And almost half of Norwich's working people have jobs in Hanover.

From town line to town line it is less than a mile; yet those who make the daily drive say it is not what links the two towns that sent them over to Vermont, but what separates them.

"I haven't spent a lot of time analyzing or justifying my own instincts, or questioning why I feel so strongly," said Deborah Muller, a member of the Norwich planning board, talking from her office at Dartmouth's Tuck School of Business. "I just feel claustrophobic over here."

Thus the commuters have breathed new life into an old debate: Vermont vs. New Hampshire, how two states that are so close geographically could be so far apart philosophically. To them, Vermont is where Yankees are hardy and contrary, yet the social welfare programs are generous. It is the state that pioneered environmental legislation—Act 250, the bottle law, the billboard ban—where people vote their convictions, ignore convention. All New Hampshire had to offer was no income tax.

Whether the distinctions are justified, or fair, they are there.

"People who live in Vermont have pretty strong feelings about it," said a Dartmouth Medical School professor, Robert Nye, who has lived in Norwich for 30 years. "You can have a cleaner conscience living in Vermont."

The first thing that struck Muller when she moved to Norwich in 1974, was visual. "Vermont's prettier," she said. "There is something about the way the roads cut through the land, the way the hills lift up."

"It's very hard to describe," said Elizabeth Ballard. She moved here in 1938, with her husband, a biology professor. "All I can say is that when you say the words 'in Vermont,' other people say 'Ahhh' and clutch their bosoms."

But it goes beyond aesthetics. "Rightly or wrongly, there is a political cast to the states," said Muller. "To the extent that you care about those things, and those of us who grew up in the '60s do still care, I identify with the politics of Vermont." Those who have made Vermont home don't mind the price. Vermont's income tax is 25.6 percent of what they pay the Internal Revenue Service.

"It's like buying a dress you really want or one that's so-so but a little cheaper," said Edye Sheier, a real estate broker. New Hampshire residents do not, in fact, come out that much ahead. What they save on earned income tax, they pay in taxes on property and unearned income. In 1983, New Hampshire collected $951 per person in state and local taxes; Vermont took $1,138. In return, according to the Council of State Governments, Vermont spends more per capita than New Hampshire on education, public welfare, health and hospitals and highways.

"My husband is a pathologist," said Jean Lawe, an editor of the *Journal of Neurosurgery* at Dartmouth. "He has said if he ever wanted to murder someone, he'd do it in New Hampshire. There's no money to spend on autopsies. We are willing to pay taxes," she said, "to get better services."

Norwich's popularity has turned it into something of an upscale anomaly in rural Vermont. In terms of family income, Norwich, population 2,473, is the fourth wealthiest town in Vermont. Median family income here is $25,313, $8,000 more than the state average.

There aren't many Vermont towns where you find a computer software consulting company, two art galleries, three restaurants, seven realty offices—and 26 lawyers, one for every 95 residents. There is even a toy lending library that lends anything from model trains for children to telescopes and computers for adults. "Toybrary" is so successful it has started franchising.

"If you were just to drive through the place and not be aware of the fact that a mile away there is a major university, you would have to look around and say, 'What is going on here?'" said James Darragh of Commercial Logic Inc., a software firm.

Not everybody feels so drawn to the Green Mountain state.

"I cannot understand the rationale," said Dennis Logue, a Dartmouth business professor. He lives in Hanover and thinks newcomers have been blinded by their own visions.

"You remember the movie *White Christmas?*" he said. "It just shows you how much people are willing to pay to live in a place they've romanticized about."

"Look what it has done to Vermont," he added. "Maybe it's all part of the politics," he said. "I'm convinced at this stage there are more social workers in Vermont than cows."

What New Hampshire and Vermont Have In Common: A Dislike of Massachusetts

by

Donna Dubuc

NEW HAMPSHIRE AND VERMONT LOOK LIKE fraternal twins to the rest of the world. But having lived in both, I can honestly say they aren't related. In New Hampshire they fight taxes; in Vermont, Wal-Marts. Vermonters elect socialists. New Hampshirites vote like Loebs. People in the Green Mountains wear funny sandals, refuse to eat their neighbors—the Holsteins—and talk about world peace. Granite Staters sell liquor at toll booths, drive without seat belts, and bear arms...or is it arm bears...just because they can. The one thing people from New Hampshire and Vermont have in common, besides a couple of rivers, is their dislike of Massachusetts.

It comes from being the Bay State's playground. Every month of the year, with the exception of two weeks in November, Interstates 89 and 93 are clogged with European sports sedans in custom colors bearing Massachusetts license plates. The cars are packed with casual clothing appropriate for aprés ski, apple picking, or antiquing. Sporting equipment of every kind is strapped to the trunk, headrest, even the antenna. They bring bikes, skis, boats, snowboards, and Tudor ice fishing huts with central air conditioning. Nothing is left behind. Reflective leg bands, waterproof wrist compasses, and collapsible chardonnay goblets are stashed into monogrammed luggage sets. These city dwellers are prepared to experience the outdoors, even if *roughing it* means staying at a bed & breakfast without a web site.

Getting up here, however, is the trick. Invariably, it means a four- or five-hour drive. Or should I say race. Everyone from Massachusetts is in a big hurry to relax.

Massachusetts drivers believe that the next four seconds of their lives are more important than the safety of yours. They ooze ego. Their children are the types to declare, "My Daddy makes more money than yours," even if they are talking to Bill Gates' son. You expect batmobile missile launchers to rise out of their hoods and vaporize your car. You can almost hear them cackle, "Take that, you post-office-box-bearing rural serf." With the urgency of a fire engine, the courage of a Kamikaze, and the persistence of a 17-year-old on his third date, Massachusetts drivers plow everyone else off the highway. If tailgating and light flashing doesn't clear a path, they'll leave tire tracks on your luggage rack. My response to highway harassment is always the same: I slow down to the speed of a tractor and watch my rearview mirror for a reaction.

"I should have bought that M1 Abrams tank when I had the chance," the Massachusetts driver says to his windshield with a far-off look on his face. "They were giving those things away after the Gulf War." He reaches for a machine gun that isn't there.

Put this same driver, however, on a back road in Vermont and he's a tour guide in Mister Rogers' neighborhood. "Look honey, a one-room schoolhouse," he says. "I'd like to see them install a metal detector in that doorway." With his eyes everywhere but on the road, he points out maple syrup taps, moos at cows in a field, and reads historic markers out loud. "Would you look at that?" he says to a sleeping wife and a teenager wearing earphones. "It's an old-fashioned general store." He turns left, then looks to see if any cars are coming. "Let's go in and buy a flannel shirt."

Tourists also stop for every stone wall, farmstand and tree that wasn't delivered in a burlap sack. Their response to a covered bridge is so quick, the only photo they take home is of their air bag inflating.

Outlet malls are another reason why Massachusetts drivers hit the brakes, but not their turn indicators (blinkers aren't standard equipment on their cars). Despite the inline skates in the trunk or the cross-country skis dividing the front and back seats, the average Massachusetts tourist spends 15 minutes recreating and 18 hours shopping during a long weekend up north.

In retail settings, tourists travel in packs like wild dogs. Six or more women from the same family fan out to take over a sale rack. You can smell the cologne and hear the demands two stores away.

"I need a new suede blazer," says a teenage girl. "Jason's seen me wear mine twice."

"Listen, princess," says Mom with a gold card in her hand. "In this family, we wear a garment six times before replacing it."

To get past a group like this in a crowded store, I simply ask, "Is that a mobile phone I hear ringing?" As they reach for their purses, I push past them.

This entire group of bargain hunters will be wearing thin, shiny jogging suits—the noisiest clothing on the market. Exercising in one of these outfits can interrupt aircraft flight patterns. In addition, they are loud in another way: the prints are the size of a wallpaper pattern in an opera house. Faux gold rope divides scenes of tropical birds, equestrian images and paisley prints. And that's just on the left sleeve.

By far the most elaborate of the weekend outfits, however, are the cyclists' uniforms. The cost of today's pedal pushers is equal to a four-year college education. These men and women look like they are competing in the Tour de France, but they are biking on Route 4 in Taftsville, Vermont.

I ran into one of these types yesterday on a narrow two-lane road. He had on a helmet that made him look like Woody Woodpecker, shoes that resembled bowling slippers, and stretch pants that looked like they had grown on him like a Chia Pet. Despite all the paraphernalia, I'm sure he wasn't a regular cyclist. He had love handles that were shaped like Volkswagen Bug wheel covers.

Oncoming traffic made it too dangerous to pass. So I hung back and hugged his rear wheel. Somehow, he looked familiar. Had he hung up the line at the lottery ticket counter by asking directions? Had he and his wife jaywalked in front of my car to get to a yard sale? Maybe he'd double parked his car next to mine at the church supper. No, I think he was one of those Massachusetts drivers who turned me into a tractor a couple of days earlier.

Since we knew each other, I wanted to make sure he safely got where he was going. I gave him an escort all the way to the Massachusetts border—flashing headlights and all. Just a little southern hospitality I learned from a neighbor.

✳ The View of Both States
✳from the Top of a Mountain

by

Tyler Resch

AN AUTUMN HIKE THAT WE UNDERTOOK to the top of Stratton Mountain in south-central Vermont recently provided not only some needed exercise but also a sense of what might be called topographical and geopolitical perspective. The panorama from the Stratton firetower at about 4,000 feet elevation on a crystal-clear day ranges from a glimpse of the Adirondacks to the northwest all the way to the Presidentials of New Hampshire to the northeast. Straight ahead to the north is Bromley Mountain with its resort housing clusters and ski trails, and then the Killington/Pico complex, plus assorted other lumps of variably hued Green Mountains beyond that. To the south, past the shimmering Somerset Reservoir and dark green ski trails on Mount Snow, one can see the highest point in Massachusetts, Mt. Greylock, along with the rest of the relaxed, lovely, but unidentifiable Berkshire Hills.

The lone summit of Mt. Monadnock in New Hampshire looms to the east, and somewhat north of that is its near-twin, Mt. Ascutney in Windsor, Vermont, which is also a "monadnock"—an isolated mountain that has resisted erosion over the eons. Nearby to the west are the familiar summits of Glastenbury Mountain with its unused firetower, and Mt. Equinox, topped with an inn and four sets of windmill blades. The whole experience, tinged with the muted colors of mid-autumn and freshened by agreeably cool winds, can be translated into words only inadequately.

We began the excursion by touching base with a tidbit of history that made us feel culturally attuned to the day's experience. Located near the start of the 2.7-mile trail up Stratton (which is a blue-blazed alternative to the Long Trail-Appalachian Trail) is a clearing identified on maps as "Webster Marker." It was here in July of 1840 that Daniel Webster reportedly addressed a crowd of 15,000 people— incredible, without benefit of a p.a. system—on behalf of the Whig candidacy of General William Henry Harrison and his running mate John Tyler (a distant ancestor of ours). Little has been recorded about the substance of what was said on the occasion, but an unforgettably good book, *The Tamarack Tree*, by Howard Breslin, published by McGraw-Hill in 1946, interwove these geographical and political elements into a historical novel; and the event has become one of the legendary chapters of Vermont history.

On a stone placed a few years ago by officials of the town of Stratton are carved the words that describe the essential facts of the episode 145 years ago. Nearby are trees that are presumably descended from the tamarack under which Daniel Webster spoke to the Whigs who had come by horse-drawn vehicles from all over the Northeast to attend a Whig convention. And it might be noted that the road leading to this clearing, known locally as the Kelley Stand, is probably in much the same condition today as it was in 1840. That is, it's a mostly unpaved holdout against the modern transportation system, complete with remnants of lateral corduroy-road logs lying across its surface. In the 1840s the Kelley Stand was probably as good a road as one would find anywhere. Today it's a beautiful anachronism, and we hope it is never "improved."

Back on the Stratton firetower steps, one is humbled by the ability to see not only much of one entire state but also portions of several others. From that vantage point one can see well beyond the narrow southern end of Vermont, and one wonders how much more elevation would be necessary to encompass the wide stretch of New Hampshire in order to see the Atlantic Ocean. All that visible geography was still making its impression on our mind's eye the next day when *The New York Times* carried an article on one of our favorite subjects, a comparison of Vermont and New Hampshire. It quoted Robert Frost, who lived in both states, speaking about the way they appear on maps: "They lie like wedges, thick end to thin end and thin end to thick end." A cartoon depicted the mirror-image states that seem so much alike and are so different.

For the benefit of those who don't know—and also for those who live here or do know but enjoy being reminded—it is a fact that Vermont and New Hampshire, so united-looking on paper, are totally different by any measurement one might make. To start with geology, New Hampshire is properly named the Granite State for its subsoil base, chunks of which are evident almost everywhere. Vermont has considerable granite, too, but most of its surface is the soft, worn-down limestone of the Appalachian chain, covered now to an extent of nearly 80 per cent with forest. New Hampshire is blessed with a goodly number of natural lakes, but in Vermont, aside from Champlain and Memphremagog, there are few lakes. All the ones we swim in each summer are manmade: Whitingham, Somerset, Woodford, Paran, Shaftsbury.

Historically, it is always worth noting that Vermont was never anyone's colony. After Europeans arrived, its status long remained that of sparsely settled woodlands caught in a political dispute between New Hampshire and New York. Vermont emerged by asserting its own independence as a Republic and stayed that way for fourteen years before it was allowed to be the first state to join the Union of the original thirteen.

Politically, New Hampshire has long been known as a heartland for vigilant right-wingism. Possibly that is painting things with a brush of too broad a stroke, but publishers like the late William Loeb and politicians like Meldrim Thomson have served to give the place a certain outrageous flavor. The drumbeat in New Hampshire has been to keep state taxes and services low while honoring a tradition of strong local control. Vermont may be known as a Republican state (though three of its last five governors have been Democrats), but most Vermont politicians who become known nationally are of a liberal bent: Warren Austin, Ralph Flanders, George Aiken, James Jeffords, Patrick Leahy. Local

control is weighty in Vermont, too, especially in public education, but it bends to the greater good in important matters
such as land-use controls and anti-billboard laws. Vermont is
a relatively high-tax state and was among the first to adopt
the progressive income tax, though among the last to suc-
cumb to a sales tax. New Hampshire proudly imposes neither
kind of tax, depending as it does on "sin" taxes paid mostly
by Massachusetts residents for liquor, cigarettes, and racing.

Industrially, New Hampshire has been heavily factory-ori-
ented, while Vermont has been more agrarian. Those lines
are blurring somewhat these days, however, as high-tech
firms respond to the interests of their employees in living
away from metropolitan regions, and a densely populated
location for business becomes less important.

Both states are heavily dependent now on the ski and sec-
ond-home economy, though Vermont guides this kind of
development with attention to aesthetic and environmental
controls, while New Hampshire operates with laissez-faire
policies—and billboards. A memorable quote on the subject
recently appeared in a modest book of photographs titled
Vermonters (Countryman Press, 1985). Speaking is John
Coolidge, resident of Plymouth, Vermont, and son of
Calvin: "I think the people in Vermont differ from the people in New Hampshire. I kid my New Hampshire friends by
telling them the only good thing about New Hampshire is
the view you get of Vermont. To which, of course, they take
exception."

The subject of the differences between these states could
go on at some length, and somebody could write a good
book about it—maybe it should be a book with two authors
and two parts, one written from each state's point of view,

because it's not easy to be impartial. The broader subject of state government is one that is widely neglected in our society and especially in our schools. Perhaps more people should climb mountains that offer them a point of view.

☀ Driving on New
☀ Hampshire's Roads

by

Tom Durgin

IT'S A GOOD THING YOUR BRAINS work fast enough to keep your head level, because driving in frost-heave-pothole-pavement-tilting season would otherwise be impossible.

There are some stretches of road where my brain works just barely fast enough. Route 10 in New Hampshire between Piermont and River Road in Haverhill is one example—its surface resembles that of a large lake in a 20-knot breeze, except that lakes don't have potholes.

New Hampshire was one of the first states to start paving roads, back in 1909. Unfortunately, those first highway engineers put down pavement over whatever the glaciers left lying about 10,000 years ago, and their successors have apparently continued the practice.

A prime example is Route 118 between Warren and Route 112 west of Woodstock. Should you ever have occasion to drive it, bring your tools and a picnic lunch, and pack the Dramamine. Highway crews leave the "frost heave" signs up well into June, and it's only partly due to a sense of humor.

Another exciting stretch of scenic highway is Route 116 between North Haverhill and Route 112. While on it recently, headed for a day of skiing, I happened upon a section where the heaves are so spectacular that you have to crawl through them—and over and around them—in second gear. When you can ski the bumps faster than you can drive them, it's time to find an alternate route.

Of course, frost heaves are only part of the adventure. Some roads look like they've been used for mortar practice.

Experienced drivers develop what I call the "New Hampshire Twitch" on pothole-infested roads. A pothole looms, and with an expert and subtle twitch of the wheel, it is deftly avoided. Sometimes, of course, a driver has to make a choice—miss the big pothole, hit the little one—and sometimes a driver has no choice.

River Road in Lyme is a good place to practice the "Twitch", although I try to avoid it this time of year. It's a scenic route, but in pothole season there's precious little time to admire the scenery.

A shock-busting, rim-bending pothole looms. Large enough to swallow a small sun, it is orbited by a system of planetary potholes. My "spaceship" suddenly seems to be taking up too much space. I Twitch, Twitch again, then execute a Double Twitch. I miss the most expensive potholes ("That'll be $177.56 Mr. Durgin," I imagine the service manager saying) but rumble over the lesser ones. They, and hundreds more like them, will eventually add up to a new set of shocks.

When a short section of New Hampshire road is in a particularly bad state of disrepair due to winter weather, highway crews put up a sign that says "Road Repairs Ahead." This is patently untrue—there's usually nothing that can be done until warmer weather—but the idea, I've been told, is to make the tourists think that there might be big trucks looming around the bend, and so slow down. Locals know enough to slow down anyway.

I don't mean to pick on New Hampshire, where I live, because a lot of the bad roads can be attributed to nature. The state has very little of what could be called "soil." For some reason, the last glacial period left the state covered with huge boulders in the north and west and sand everywhere else. Neither base is suitable for roads.

In fact, the disparity between the heavy, granitic north and west and the lighter, sandy southeast may cause hidden and powerful distortions that make the roads even worse. The dividing line between heavy and light—I bet you didn't know this—passes right through Franklin, near the epicenter of a couple of mild earthquakes in recent years.

And that demonstrates the real problem. The natural tendency of New Hampshire, due to the weight disparity, is to tilt toward Vermont. If it did, the strain would be greatly relieved. But as we all know, New Hampshire tilts toward the right.

Vermont Drivers: Good Luck!

by

Eric Roode

I USED TO LIVE IN CLAREMONT, NEW HAMPSHIRE—quite close to the Vermont border—and it seemed that every time I was stuck behind a terminally slow driver, it had the familiar white-on-green license plate. Vermont drivers are amazingly slow.

Also, I have come to the conclusion that it is a state law in Vermont that if you are on a side road and you see a car approaching at a high rate of speed, you must pull out in front of the car, and subsequently drive at ten miles per hour below the speed limit.

I came to this conclusion—and a friend from Maine corroborated—during many drives to Albany, New York via Route 9 in Vermont, which is a twisty mountainous road that has looooong stretches of no-passing zones. Sometimes up to 15 miles of no-passing zones. Do you have any idea what it's like to drive behind Grandma Moses for 15 miles?

The only other semi-amusing thing about Vermonters is that the parking lot at the Claremont Wal-Mart was always filled with cars with Vermont license plates.

New Hampshire is the best state of the fifty in which to live, although I must admit that Vermont is hardly the worst—it's not even the worst state in New England in which to live.

CHAPTER

FIVE

The Gloves Come Off

F ifty-ish guy in Porsche says to Woodsville, New Hampshire, bookstore proprietor, David Major: "We're looking for the real Vermont. I figured a guy like you should know."

Major: "Well, for one thing, you're in New Hampshire."

The guy's trophy wife: "I hear Woodstock is a charming town."

Major: "Yes, I think you should go there."

—With thanks to *It's Classified's* Tom Durgin's well-honed eye.

Why I Hate New Hampshire

by

Mike Barnicle

RECENTLY, I HAD THE OPPORTUNITY to visit Vermont and New Hampshire. My trips again reminded me of the incredible differences between two states many assume are similar.

On paper, according to the census, they appear to be a match: Vermont has half a million people, making it 49th of 50 states in population. The median age for residents is 33. It is 98 percent white and has a 5 percent unemployment rate.

New Hampshire has about a million residents. That places it 40th in rank. It, too, is 98 percent white and also has an unemployment rate lingering around 5 percent.

This proves beyond doubt that statistics are stupid. As a matter of fact, two states could not be more different.

Vermont is a beautiful place, a postcard. New Hampshire looks like Arkansas with snow.

Vermont was home to Abe Lincoln's son and the von Trapp family. New Hampshire gave us the lunatic publisher

Loeb, the thief Sherman Adams, the preposterous Sununu and a member of the Manson gang.

Vermont passed a Clean Air act before the environment became trendy. New Hampshire wrote a constitutional amendment raising the IQ of its citizens by 50 points so they could communicate with their house pets.

Vermont has several nifty towns like Brattleboro and Montpelier. New Hampshire's largest city—Manchester—has a main street that concludes at a dead end.

First thing you see when you cross into Vermont is spectacular foliage and sprawling valleys that recede into picturesque, rolling hills. First thing you see in New Hampshire is a toll booth where the attendant is stumped making change for a $5 bill, followed by a state liquor store.

They speak English in Vermont. They speak a contorted form of gibberish in New Hampshire, saying things like, "Geez-o crow, look 'hup the street, the soldiers are marching down."

Vermont has a lot of extremely attractive women. In New Hampshire, the best-looking females are those who trim their mustaches.

Vermont is a mecca for tourists. New Hampshire attracts illiterate ice fishermen and motorcycle gangs.

Vermont has two capable United States senators. New Hampshire has Judd Gregg, a complete dope who won the 1993 Anthony Perkins "Psycho" look-alike contest and took great pride in the fact he tried to take a dying woman's money after she put a down payment on his property and then tried to get it back after she contracted cancer. When

Gregg announced for the Senate, they coined the phrase, "The sap is running."

On Saturday evenings in Vermont, residents go out to eat or stay home to listen to that boring screwball on National Public Radio. Saturday nights in New Hampshire there is a debate over whether to bathe for the week ahead.

Vermont has a lot of people who moved from Massachusetts and New York to escape the rat race. New Hampshire has thousands who moved in out of pure self-ishness, to avoid taxes or doing anything that might help a neighbor.

In Vermont, if you get sick they take you to a hospital. In New Hampshire, if you become ill, old or infirm they use you for fertilizer or target practice.

In Vermont, people sometimes complain about the cold of winter or the mud in spring. In New Hampshire, the most common complaint is the sheep either have a headache or they lie.

To be fair, New Hampshire does have some good points. Areas like Portsmouth, Keene and Peterborough and places like Dartmouth and Durham get a special exemption because they don't fit with the rest of the state. In addition, New Hampshire has a lot of funerals.

Vermont is called the "Green Mountain State." New Hampshire has "Live Free or Die" on its license plates and the Legislature would actually prefer three of the words be removed so the slogan would simply read, "Die."

Vermonters are urbane and fashionable in a rural-chic way. Granite State natives are a mentally-challenged lot of easily confused white people who think buildings with elevators qualify as tourist attractions and spend enormous amounts of money in tattoo parlors or gun stores.

When people from Vermont take a vacation, they travel to spots like Yellowstone Park or Sanibel Island. In New Hampshire, they get in their snowmobiles or speed boats and go to motels to take pictures of indoor plumbing.

Vermont is comfortable and progressive. New Hampshire is home to oddballs in Day-Glo hats, with a deer tossed on top of their truck who pride themselves in being sour, stingy sociopaths who revel in the economic misery of others.

Vermont is New England. In New Hampshire, even the Old Man of the Mountain wants out.

✸ More of Why I Hate New Hampshire

by

Mike Barnicle, again

WELL, THE SAP IS RUNNING AGAIN in New Hampshire And this year's principal dope is a rich guy named Steve Forbes who might as well issue bumper stickers reading: "Putz for President."

Take a peek at this goober! He's a goofy-looking millionaire trying to sell something called a flat tax in a state where the average IQ of most Republicans over 35 resembles the flat line at the far right-hand corner of the bell curve.

If you removed just four regions from the Granite State— Portsmouth, Concord, Keene and Hanover—the entire place would be a sit-com starring Buddy Ebsen, Chill Wills, Pat Buttram and Pee-Wee Herman. Maybe toss in Michael Jackson too because he is both white and slow.

But Forbes seems to have found a receptive audience for his ludicrous proposal because New Hampshire ranks 50th out of all states in charitable contributions. It's "Live free or die" up there and the latter option costs nothing, so people are constantly encouraged to simply keel over dead before they bother anyone for help.

Unfortunately, it's more than likely this will be the last time New Hampshire will play an inflated role in presidential elections on the flimsy grounds that it holds the nation's first primary. By the year 2000, everyone will be interactive as well as on-line and voters will select candidates in a national primary at half-time of the Rose Bowl.

Oddly enough, this will be sad.

New Hampshire, for all its horrendous defects and strong claim to being the most selfish, self-absorbed state in the Union, is kind of cute. And every four years, it is fun to see the national media treat it like a lab experiment.

Many reporters are struck by the fact that a spring training game between the Texas Rangers and New York Mets moves at a faster pace than the mind of the average Granite State resident. (According to the Census Bureau, New Hampshire leads the nation in the number of residents who majored in driver ed, as well as children named after popular household appliances.) So, it's easy to take notes up there. Why, you can even stop for a mocha latte in between jotting down verbs.

The pace of life in New Hampshire also serves as a refreshing contrast to the dog-eat-brie existence the media get used to in East Coast cities. There, they are hounded with questions like, "Where do you work? How much do you make? Who do you know?" but in New Hampshire people are unassuming, quaintly aloof and the most they ever say is, "Nice tooth."

In Washington, reporters constantly try to one-up each other by claiming to have more contacts or better sources. In New Hampshire, they one-up each other by driving bigger snowmobiles to reserved ice-fishing holes where they sit for days in bizarre outfits that look like they were once owned by Arsenio Hall.

The Forbes campaign fits right in. It does not require even the most minimal human contact—a handshake or a smile—because it's all on TV. The entire campaign, all 30 seconds, is right there in the middle of "Jeopardy."

Yet it appeals to those most basic human emotions, the elements that compel hundreds to register Republican and establish residence in New Hampshire: collective greed and individual selfishness. No income taxes. No welfare drain. No need for a conscience.

Forbes acquired his immense wealth the way Granite State Republicans admire and envy: First, he was born and then his father croaked, leaving him more cash than you'll find in the state treasury in Concord.

The old man, Malcolm Forbes, was quite a character. He dressed like the owner of a Provincetown leather bar, rode motorcycles, flew hot air balloons, had picnics in France that cost more than the Clinton's legal bills and amassed a huge fortune that his son, "Thanksdad," is using to campaign with.

The son is also an unusual piece of work. He is a perfect dweeb, the kind of guy who was pounded to a pulp by classmates every day of his pathetic, privileged grammar school life and looks today as if he could not cross the street without first sipping a nice cup of Metamucil.

Perhaps the only redeeming virtue of "Mr. Pocket-Protector's" presidential ambition is it is killing that total moron Phil Gramm. Gomer Pyle is going down for the count in New Hampshire, beaten by a millionaire actually running for the post of top accountant.

The whole thing is perfect: The curtain is dropping on the Granite State's quadrennial moment in the pale sun and the pageant this time features a wealthy nerd whose only pitch is an echo of the state's motto: "What about me?"

Reasons for Hating Vermont

by

Donald Hall

VERMONTERS LEAD QUIET, INTROSPECTIVE lives among the unspoiled splendors of their countryside, interrupted only by brunches, cocktail parties, and Masterpiece Theatre. Vermont invented the Young Rural Professional in 1974; in the same year, the yuppie invented Vermont. But it is not true that Vermonters live a serene existence without worries of any kind. The editor of a distinguished country journal once wrote a column about a typical Vermont dilemma. Which was better for starting the fire in your woodstove, he pondered, the *New York Times* or the *Wall Street Journal?*

New Hampshire is inhabited by real people who drive pickup trucks with gun racks and NRA bumper stickers; Vermont is a theme park full of Bostonians, New Yorkers, and Nebraskans dressed up in Vermont suits. When writers, intellectuals, violinists, and CEOs live north of Boston, they live in Vermont. If the oboe from the Indianapolis Symphony keeps a summer place back East, will it be a cottage on Lake

Sunapee? If the chair of the mathematics department at Texas A & M drives five mornings into the sun from College Station for the month of August, does he aim for Penacook? In August, Vermont drones with the sound of string quartets while motorcycle gangs converge on Laconia. (The rest of the year in New Hampshire it's the same noise, now performed by chainsaws and snowmachines.) Music festivals in Green Mountain towns, common as church suppers in New Hampshire, attract professors from the University of America, wearing checked shirts out of the L. L. Bean catalogue. Saturday mornings, while a native takes his trash to the dump, the collegial hayseed ties his Volvo to the old hitching post and swaps stories with the salty character who runs the general store this summer, who last year managed Kuala Lumpur for IBM.

In the 1995 census it was discovered that seventeen indigenous Vermonters remained in the state; twelve spent their winters in Florida with their running-to-the-dump money. The rest had migrated to New Hampshire, from Malltown to Milltown.

Meantime, in the world at large, a conspiracy denies New Hampshire's existence and implies that Vermont borders Maine. Vermont has become the generic name for any place north of Boston, unless it's got lobsters. At poetry readings I find myself invariably introduced as resident of an old family farm in Vermont. Five hundred people have written me letters, correctly addressed, in which they asked me how the weather was up there in Vermont. Twelve visitors have written us notes, after a week or a weekend, saying how much they enjoyed visiting us in Vermont.

In Vermont deer are required to have shots. In Vermont people keep flocks of spayed sheep to decorate their lawns. In Vermont when inch-long trout are released into streams, a state law requires that they be preboned and stuffed with wild rice delicately flavored with garlic and thyme. Vermont has decorator barns; Calvin Klein will sign your woodshed for $50,000. In Vermont you can buy boots precaked with odorless manure. Taylor Rental outside Burlington hires Yankees out for parties, each guaranteed to know three hundred amusing rural anecdotes, all of them ending, "You can't get there from here." They chew nylon straw, they repeat "Ayuh" over and over again, and they cackle hideously until you pay them off. In 1998 TransUniversal Corporation acquired Vermont, reorganized it as Yankeeworld, and moved it to Arizona on flatbed tractors.

In New Hampshire the state supper is beans and franks, and every recipe begins with salt pork, Campbell's Cream of Mushroom, and Miracle Whip. In New Hampshire breakfast and supper are both at five o'clock. In New Hampshire a brunch is something not to walk into when you are hunting coon. In New Hampshire convenience stores sell Fluff, Wonder Bread, Moxie, and shoes with blue canvas tops. In Vermont they have the forty-hour work week; in New Hampshire the forty-hour work weekend is standard. In New Hampshire people work a hundred hours a week cutting wood, setting up the yard sale, and misdirecting flatlanders; the rest of the time they make Vermont maple syrup and Vermont cheese.

Vermonters who commute from Brookline in BMWs call New Hampshire folk rednecks. (**Redneck**, n., commonly used by liberals and college graduates to describe people who can drive a nail.) Patten Corporation completed paving Vermont in 1947.

It is true that parts of New Hampshire have already defected to other states: Salem is a suburb of Boston; Nashua is Silicon Valley with frost heaves; Winnipesaukee has been Coney Island for as long as Coney Island; Waterville Valley is a component of Aspen. It is true that we used to have a governor who wanted to nuke Massachusetts. It is true that New Hampshire is known nationally only for its early primary and its Live Free or Die license plate. Once every four years a New Hampshire citizen has a fifty-fifty chance to be interviewed on national television, and we are the only state so far to fulfill Andy Warhol's prophecy about everybody being famous for fifteen minutes. Once every four years the *New York Times, Time, Newsweek,* and *USA Today* send reporters to the Ramada Inn in Concord to file stories about desolation, political rigidity, fecklessness, and stale hors d'oeuvres.

New Hampshire's license plate motto comes from a revolutionary war hero, General John Stark, who may have been thinking more of Massachusetts than of George III. New Hampshire's obnoxious and independent bloody-mindedness derives from the seventeenth century, when the Bay Colony, sometimes abetted by London, tried to eat it alive. It derives also from the eighteenth, nineteenth, and twentieth centuries, as Massachusetts continues to cast cannibal glances north. Like the rural South, New Hampshire lives in a present that is the product of its history, and American history still lives in New Hampshire genes; mind you, we still vote for Frank Pierce.

Franklin Pierce, if you never noticed, was the fourteenth president of the United States, the only president from New Hampshire, and incidentally the only one not to be renominated by his own party after his term in office. If Rodney Dangerfield were authentic—and did not vacation in Las Vegas, Vermont—he would be Franklin Pierce. Vermont's only president, on the other hand, was Calvin Coolidge, elected to the highest office because, as governor of Massachusetts, he suppressed strikes.

In Vermont the state flower is the sushi bar, and the state bird is the electric hot tub. In New Hampshire the state lunch is a submarine sandwich with a tub of coleslaw. Both are manufactured in the great coleslaw factories of Secaucus off the New Jersey Turnpike. Twenty-three years after his death, Robert Frost remains the poet laureate of Vermont; like the rest of Yankeeland decoration, this poet laureate no longer functions, but he sure is cute. In Vermont, the license plate slogan was Eat Three Nutritious Meals a Day. In legislative committee this slogan edged out Experience Mozart.

Vermont plays double-A baseball in IBM's Burlington, as New Hampshire features the Nashua Pirates just off El Camino Real. But genuine New Hampshire folks play in the major leagues. Rich Gale won two games last year in Japan's World Series; he grew up in Littleton, with an effective summer season of thirty-eight days, counting Sundays. Still in the majors are Mike Flanagan, pitching for the Orioles, who like Kansas City's Steve Balboni comes from Manchester; Joe Lefebvre of the Phillies, from Concord; and the great Carlton Fisk, most New Hampshire character of all, who grew up in the small Connecticut River town of Charlestown. It is rumored that one Vermonter clings to the roster of the California Angels.

Not far north of Carlton Fisk's Charlestown, west and across the river, is Woodstock, Vermont, which just now lacks a representative in the major leagues. Woodstock is why I hate Vermont—and what I fear for New Hampshire. This is the Woodstock that Rockefeller money embalmed in the shroud of a small New England town: instant "Ye" at every parking lot; cute boutiques elbowing each other down main street; a dear old country inn fabricated in 1969. Nostalgia without history is a decorative fraud, and condosaurus, having consumed Vermont, munches at New Hampshire's borders.

✽　✽　✽

This story originally appeared in the now-defunct magazine, *New England Monthly,* which received five hundred and seven letters, all postmarked Vermont, indignantly reminding me that Chester A. Arthur was born in Fairfield, Vermont, on October 5, 1830. Actually it was 1831. Like many Vermonters, he became a New York machine politician.

Also, in 1989, Galway Kinnell was named Vermont State Poet. We understand that Professor Kinnell lives on Bleecker Street in Greenwich Village.

✦ A Good Fight With a Long History

by

Lisa Shaw

SOMETIMES IT SEEMS THAT THE MOST popular pastime in New Hampshire is Rag on Vermont.

And vice versa.

"Vermont is full of old hippies and flatlanders whose idea of slumming is ordering a Catamount beer without the glass."

"Oh yeah? When disabled people in New Hampshire need some help from the state government, they're asked to take a number."

Once when I wrote an article about Vermont in a newsletter for people who want to move from the city to the country, the line that easily caused the most commotion was: "I know why people chose to live there (Vermont), and I know why others—like me—don't." Why?

Okay, I'll tell you. First, a caveat: some of you aren't going to like what I'm going to say. When I lived in New York and dreamed of moving out, Vermont was the first and only thing on my mind. I had visited and traveled through the state, but there was just something about the aura of the place that stirred me. And the travel pages of the *Times* and other papers that I read rarely wrote about New Hampshire; always, it was Vermont. *Vermont Magazine* and *Vermont Life*, as well as the articles about the state that came out in *Harrowsmith Country Life* just added to my fixation on the place.

And so I first landed in Barnard, Vermont in March of 1988, eyes wide at the whole prospect of living in the Green Mountain State. Unfortunately, Barnard is just north of Woodstock, which is about the most crowded small town in the state ten months out of the year. That's not what I moved out of New York for, and so a few months later I headed across the river to Lebanon, New Hampshire, an affordable apartment my only goal; it didn't matter which side of the Connecticut River I was on. I ended up living a few miles from Dartmouth. Once I had a 603 area code, I discovered that this part of New Hampshire didn't attract the tourists that Vermont did. It also had more of a small-town feel, again without the intrusiveness that tourism now brings to all corners of Vermont.

Once I was living in an area that didn't rely economically on tourism, I began to examine the other differences between the states. My area, the Upper Valley, is a twin-state region, so many times I've found it to be impossible to attend a party or barbecue without someone bringing up the myriad differences between the two states. It happened again the other day when we were in a coffee shop in Windsor, Vermont. The Vermont guy was picking on the

New Hampshire couple about property taxes and auto insurance. He thought they were both twice as much as Vermont (they're not), but the New Hampshirities were fighting a losing battle in trying to convince him.

Yes, Vermont is pretty—as is New Hampshire—but here's why I live in the Granite State.

The tax structure is better. Property taxes might be more here, but we don't have to pay either sales tax or state income tax. That helps a lot.

Look at the phone book: Vermont government takes up a page and a half; New Hampshire's listings take up less than one column, a result of the decreased revenue structure that flows to Concord. Of course there are problems, but it works. Vermont is also renowned as a great place for people to be on welfare, and I've heard many people who live in towns along its borders complain about people from away who move into the state just to get higher welfare checks. And sorry, but does Vermont really need a state archaeologist? Your tax dollars at work...

Yes, New Hampshire certainly has its share of blowhard politicians, but on the state level I think our small form of government works well. If you haven't noticed, it's getting a lot of notice from the national press due to our status as the first primary state. But everyone I know is already sick of the Tom, Dick & Harry candidates who traipse their way through the state spitting platitudes more often than not. The best bumper sticker I've seen is: "This must be New Hampshire if every other person you meet is running for president."

Rabid environmentalists won't agree with me, but the strict, almost unreasonable environmental regulations in

Vermont are bad for business. Even though I run a tiny business, if I want to add another building to my land I can do it by just getting a permit from the town clerk. In Vermont, I'd have to go through countless rounds of presentations to get the same plan accepted, if in fact, they decide to go along with it. Yes, I know that some parts of New Hampshire are overbuilt, but that's the price we pay for the right to do what we want with the land we own. Live Free or Die is the most appropriate motto this state could ever have, and I subscribed to it even when I was living in New York and New Jersey. Too bad it didn't mean anything back there.

People kid about Vermont being a Socialist State with Bernie Sanders and the progressive government that rules in Burlington, but because of this Vermont tends to attract ultra-politically correct people who are into being PC to see how many nits they can pick, I feel. Maybe I've just gotten a bit conservative as I've gotten older—running a business and living in the Granite State have also contributed to this feeling—because I'm generally not a grouch. But people who love being PC just love Vermont. I just feel that by the time you get through allowing everyone their space to air their thoughts and feelings, and then time for another round while you go around the feelings circle another time so that everyone has a chance to offer and receive feedback, well, you may be full of warm fuzzies, but you haven't accomplished a damn thing. And the farmers, and the other natives of Vermont—the people who have roots in the state and can talk your ears off with great stories—won't give you the time of day if you subscribe to this belief.

As one person from Washington, DC put it to me a couple of weeks ago, "Well, I never hear anyone say that they

want to move to New Hampshire." Not true, and I regularly talk to people who want to know about the different parts
of New Hampshire and how they're different from each
other. Vermont gets lumped into *Vermont*, when people start
to get misty-eyed over the prospect of moving there even
though the southwest corner has absolutely nothing in common with the Northeast Kingdom. I've experienced the following geographic desires to move: New Yorkers want to go
to Vermont, people in the Boston area want to move to
Maine, and people from Connecticut want to move to New
Hampshire. I talk to a lot of people, and this makes sense:
it's almost as if they follow a straight line to their intended
destinations; to divert from these paths takes a bit more
effort, they must imagine.

If you count the mile markers on the interstate until
you're finally over the border to your desired state and you
get off in the first town you see, you're not alone. My only
warning is to not jump blindly. Take off the blinders when it
comes to your attitudes towards Vermont and against other
states.

CHAPTER

SIX

An Uneasy Truce

*T*hough a polygraph test might reveal that average Vermonters regard their neighbors across the Connecticut River as cavemen, their progressive state historically takes its cue from conservative New Hampshire in presidential primaries. In the 80s, when Vermont's primary was not binding, the Republican victor in New Hampshire won there, too.

—Rich Barlow,
Valley News reporter, in the wake of
Pat Buchanan's win in the 1996 New Hampshire primary.

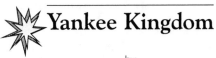

Yankee Kingdom

by

Ralph Nading Hill

IT MAY SURPRISE YOU THAT NOWHERE in the United States is the democratic ideal more fully embodied in government and in the life of the people than in these two tiny American states (Vermont and New Hampshire) tucked away up east under the Canadian border. According to Viscount James Bryce, a former ambassador to the United States from your native England:

> You men of northern Vermont and northern New Hampshire, living among its rocks and mountains in a region which may be called the Switzerland of America—you are the people here who have had hearts full of love of freedom which exists in mountain people, and who have the indomitable spirit and the unconquerable will which we always associate with the lake and mountain lands of the Alps and Scotland.

It is noble country from the Isles of Shoals and the tidal inlets of the Piscataqua 200 miles west over the mountains to glimmering Champlain. The whole is rich in human experience and in meaning not only because, in the words of de Tocqueville, it is here that "democracy finds a more judicious choice than it does elsewhere," but because in the wild tempo of the present day it is one of the truly civilized places in which to live.

Traveling north through the Champlain Valley not long ago two men fell to discussing what one of them called the "myth" of Vermont. "You are talking of a Vermont that once was, but no longer is," declared the driver.

"Look around you," answered his friend, a native of the Green Mountains. "What makes you think this is any less beautiful than it was a hundred years ago?" He waved toward the gentle green hills and the lake bathed in sunshine and the blue Adirondacks beyond.

"Right here, yes. But Burlington and Rutland are no more the old Vermont than Manchester and Nashua are the old New Hampshire. All right, I'll grant that the small towns are pretty much the same. What I'm talking about is the people—all the stories about the old-time Yankee."

The fact that a people so homogeneous (they were more than 90 percent English or of English descent) could develop such different views in a relatively small area can partially be explained by geography. The White and Green Mountain ranges set the people apart. Even today it is possible to distinguish by their accents natives who live east of the Green Mountains from those of the west.

Someone has remarked that if Vermont were flattened out it would be as large as Texas. Its forested peaks, bowed like veterans of old wars, parade in broken ranks 157 miles all the way from Massachusetts to Canada. Although none of the Green Mountain or Taconic ranges aspire to Mount Washington's 6,288 feet, or quite to the commanding mile reached by its five other rugged companions in New Hampshire's Presidential Range, Vermont is much the more mountainous of the two states. It is the most mountainous state in the Union.

As the mammoth ice sheet ground southward a million years ago, enveloping even the highest peaks in its brutal grip, it somehow carried away less soil from Vermont than from New Hampshire; and when finally it melted back into the Arctic it dropped less stone on the Green Mountain State. Because of this and of the way the mountains were formed, Vermonters found a livelihood in nearly every remote valley. Vermont is less industrial because geography so widely scatters its people. New Hampshire is less agrarian because the White Mountains are high and jagged and because their blanket of boulders and stones is so heavy that the land in many places has never been reclaimed.

Early in the nineteenth century Granite State people began to congregate in the mill cities of flat lands to the southeast. Yet there are areas in both states in which a native, upon removal of a blindfold would be at a loss to tell whether he was in Vermont or New Hampshire. On both sides of the Connecticut River one sees the same wrinkled hills and steepled villages. There are those who swear that Vermont is greener, which it may be because of soil and topography, and that they can tell the difference the moment they cross the border. But to the stranger it is very much all one countryside. The people of the rural areas, at least, seem to be very much the same, which indeed they should be since they all came from the same Yankee stock.

They have the same outlook—the outlook of mountain people.

While Vermont and New Hampshire have aptly been called twin states, they are not identical. Their differences, however, are not as easily counted as their similarities. Vermont is thought of as rural and New Hampshire as industrial, yet Vermont has considerable industry and New Hampshire has hundreds of square miles of rural countryside.

There is no denying the fact that if one's main object in life is to make money the New Hampshire and Vermont hill country is a hard place to do it, but there are other values that return equivalent dividends. The North Country has been fortunate in gaining the services in its academics and hospitals, for example, of teachers and doctors it could not afford except in terms of these other values. One reason that the Mary Hitchcock Clinic in Hanover and the Mary Fletcher Medical Center in Burlington are outstanding is that able young doctors and specialists in various fields who twenty-five years ago might have gone to New York or Boston would now rather live and practice in moderately populated communities near rivers, lakes and mountains, with summer and winter recreational facilities for their families—communities that have universities with medical schools and well-equipped hospitals and laboratory facilities. The deeper we go into the atomic era the greater these attractions may become. The one-way road of emigration out of the hill country has been a long one, but even the longest road turns eventually.

How much credit can be given New Hampshire and Vermont towns and villages for having resisted the temptation to have plastic surgery done on their streets and houses is a question. Not having suffered city real estate pressures to tear down, to rebuild and to modernize they have thus far succeeded.

Any North Country concern that wants to stay independent had better not be too rich or too poor. If too rich it is in danger of being plucked off the vine by city capitalists and having the juice squeezed out of it. If it has debt it is likely to be bought merely for the carry-over of its losses as a tax benefit for a large company in a high income bracket. Of course some native concerns that otherwise would have gone out of business have been saved by the very bigness that has ruined their neighbors. By becoming part of a larger enterprise with much better marketing facilities they have prospered as never before. But such companies are in danger of losing the character they had when locally owned, for the decisions are made in big cities, often without regard for local interests and welfare.

New Hampshire industry has survived various economic cataclysms with surprising vigor and is responsible today for the modest growth of the state's population—while Vermont has gained more slowly. Presumably the moral of this is that if Vermont wants to grow it should have more industry. It could use more, comfortably, but if it had as much as New Hampshire its character might change and that, to its tens of thousands of admirers, would be a loss hard to calculate.

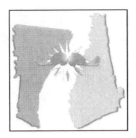

Acknowledgments

"Kittens in the Oven," by Hank Nichols, originally appeared in *The Boston Globe*. Reprinted by permission of the author.

"New Hampshire vs. Vermont," by Judson Hale. Reprinted by permission of *American Heritage Magazine*, a division of Forbes, Inc. Copyright Forbes, Inc., 1992.

Barbara Radcliffe Rogers lives in Richmond, New Hampshire, and with her husband Stillman Rogers, is co-author of *New Hampshire: Off the Beaten Path* (1995, Globe PequotPress).

"Why I Live in New Hampshire," by Judson Hale. Reprinted by permission of *American Heritage Magazine*, a division of Forbes, Inc. Copyright Forbes, Inc., 1992.

"Vermont Won't Come to You," by Peter S. Jennison. As originally appeared in *Roadside History of Vermont*, Mountain Press Publishing Company.